Am I a-Strayan?

David & Faith Weisbrot
Illustrations by Janet Mitsuji

Inspired by Bryan Weisbrot

Am I a'Strayan?
paperback ISBN 978-0-6459286-3-1
hardcover ISBN 978-0-6459286-4-8
Copyright© David & Faith Weisbrot and Janet Mitsuji (illustrations) 2023
All rights reserved.
First published 2023 by Uh-Oh Publishing

No part of this publication may be reproduced, stored in a retrieval
system, or transmitted in any form by any means electronic, mechanical,
photocopying, recording or otherwise without
the prior consent of the publishers.

Typesetting and book design by Rack and Rune Publishing
https://rackandrune.com

www.ingramcontent.com/pod-product-compliance
Lightning Source LLC
Chambersburg PA
CBRC092340290426
44109CB00008B/174